How to Play
RUNNING

Edited & Compiled by

Dr. Ravi S. Pothuvaal
B.P.Ed., M.P.Ed., NIS (Athletics), Ph.D.,
Professor (Deptt. of Physical Education & Sports)
S.R. College of Physical Education
Bengaluru (Karnataka)

PRERNA PRAKASHAN
C-13, Plot No. D-5, Rose Apartment,
Sector-14 Extension, Rohini, Delhi-110085
Phones: (Office) 011-65749511, 23240261
(Mobile) 9868028838 (Residence) 27562163
E-mail: lakshaythani@hotmail.com

Published by:

PRERNA PRAKASHAN
C-13, Plot No. D-5, Rose Apartment,
Sector-14 Extension, Rohini, Delhi-110085
Ph. : (Office) 65749511, 23240261 (Mobile) 9868028838
(Residence) 27562163 (Fax) 011-23240261
E-mail: *lakshaythani@hotmail.com*

I.S.B.N: 978-93-81867-42-6

PRINTED IN INDIA 2013

Laser Typeset by:

JAIN MEDIA GRAPHICS,
C-8/77-B, Keshav Puram, Delhi-35

Printed by:

VISHAL KAUSHIK PRINTERS, Delhi-110093

Price: Rs. 250/-

CONTENTS

1

RUNNING — AN INTRODUCTION

HISTORICAL BACKGROUND OF RUNNING

Athletics, as we know it today has been in existence for a little over 100 years. Event of Athletic is made up of various events of which Running is one of an important

constituent.

Like Athletics, Running also includes various events in it. In this chapter, we will go through these events.

The main constituents of running are as follows:

1. Sprinting
2. Hurdling
3. Middle Distance Running
4. Relay Racing,
5. Steeplechase,

Brief introduction of all these events have been mentioned step by step below:

SPRINTING

One is sprinting when he is running at his top speed making full effort all the way through the race from start to finish. Sprinting is as a race includes all distances up to 400 metres, with the 400 metres classified as a long spring. Races beyond 400 metres usually fall into the category of middle distance, though elite athletes may sprint much of the distance.

This is a fact that event of sprinting occurs in every race. As the competitive distance increases from the very short sprints to longer distances, so the demands on the athlete change.

In short sprints, the athlete races on stored energy supplies. As the race distance increases, so does the demand on the athlete's anaerobic capacity, and the aerobic capability beings to be taxed as well.

RUNNING

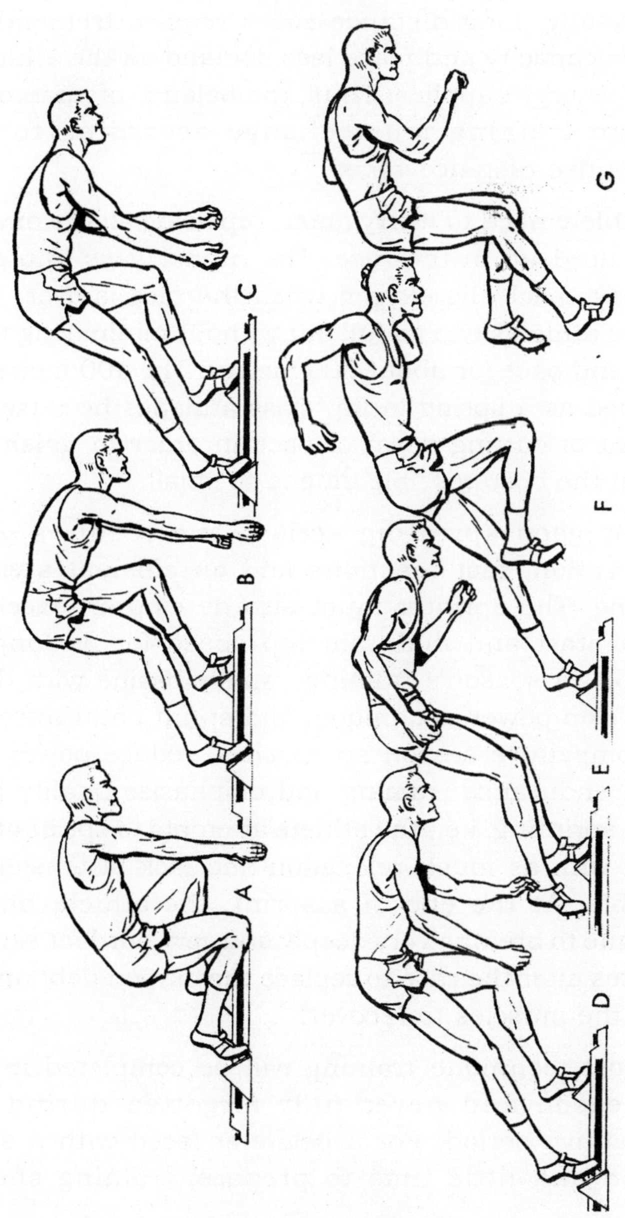

Usually, long distance races require tremendous aerobic capacity and place less demand on the athlete's stored energy supplies. Thus, the balance of anaerobic-aerobic training must change according to the competitive distance raced.

Athlete need to worry about replacing all the oxygen being used up in the race. The runner goes into debt and pays back the oxygen when the race is over. Well trained athletes can go full out without minimising their effort and pace for about 300 metres. The 400 metres is included as a spring in top class athletics because the amount of cutting down of pace in order to finish the race in the best possible time is so small.

For good sprinting action, one requires good acceleration, fast reactions and an efficient style of running. The sprinter must also develop an excellent sprint start and maintain top speed for as long as possible. A season's training usually begins with drills to develop power, technique, and sprint endurance. As the competitive season approaches, reduce power and sprint endurance training and emphasize quality high speed sprinting, i.e., the athlete attempts to sprint at top speed with as much relaxation and lack of tension as possible. At the end of a sprint, the athlete has to continue to breathe very deeply and very hard for several minutes after the race to replace the oxygen debt and to allow the muscles to recover.

Most technique training will be completed in the pre-season and never fully forgotten during the competitive period. For a beginner faced with a short season and little time to prepare, training should concentrate on improving the fundamental sprinting technique and the ability to relax while sprinting at top speed.

Some of the earliest records of running events are those of men who ran against each other at the first Olympic Games. Running was the simplest of the sports, but it too became debased as prizes and the entertainment value became more important than training and physical prowess. The sprint race was the length of the stadium and the stones which marked the start allowed for twenty runners in a heat.

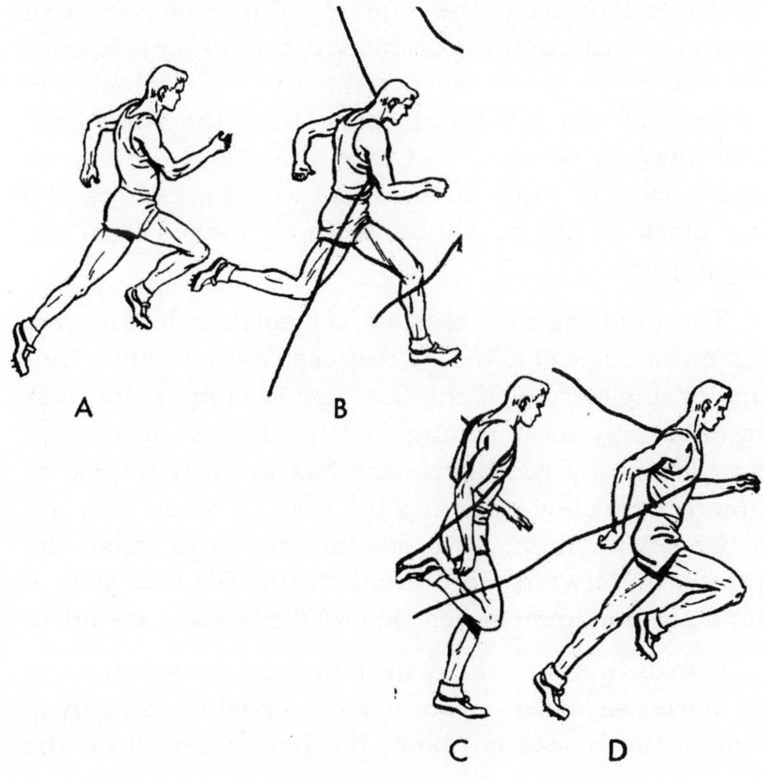

The first record of a modern meet which included sprinting was in the year 1864 when Oxford competed against Cambridge. Thus, it can be said about this event that it is not new born in world of sports and today has became a very popular event.

Sprinting Procedure

The first thing in the sprinting procedure is to set the blocks properly. The blocks should be set at the sprinter's preferred distance. It is recommended that the bunch or medium position be used by most sprinters, with the blocks 11 to 15 inches apart. If the distance of the front foot from the starting line has not been determined through experience, a beginning reference point may be found by placing the front block the distance of two full hand spans from the front line. Modification of this distance should be made as experience and study dictate. This would mean that the rear block would be about 25 to 30 inches from the starting line.

The front leg in a starting set position in the past formed an angle of about 80 degrees. It was thought that this leg angle enabled the front leg to support the rear leg effectively as it swung through for the first step. However, many good sprinters has recently tended to extend completely or nearly the rear leg when they are in the set position. This position tends to make the sprinter go forward more easily during his first step. A stand position immediately behind the block is assumed.

One or two moderately deep breaths are taken when the starter says, Go to your marks. A position directly in front of the blocks is taken, the hands placed on the ground, and the feet backed into the starting blocks, placing the first front and then the rear foot against the blocks. If sufficient training has not been experienced, it is suggested that the stronger leg be placed in front. If leg and foot strength devices, such as dynamometres, are not available, a crude method may be used to determine the stronger foot. The sprinter stands erect with both feet together. Someone gently pushes him from the rear in the small of the back. Usually he will support his weight with his stronger leg, thus stepping forward with the weaker leg in the first step.

Then the hands are dusted off and the rear knee is kept on the ground. The hands are now placed on the ground and the wrists rotated outward so that the thumb and index finger are just behind the starting line, spread and parallel. The body weight is borne on the fingers, only the finger tips and thumb tips of each hand should be in contact with the ground. The arms should hang in a perpendicular line from the shoulders to the ground, with the two thumbs about 8 inches apart.

Some sprinters may prefer to have the hands slightly wider than shoulder width. Some few even use a very wide hand spread of as much as 20 or more inches. The head should be loose, relaxed, and allowed to hang down. At the command set, one quick breath may be taken before the body weight moves upward and forward over the hands, so that all that is necessary is to pull the hands out to the side to start to fall forward. The legs then move fast enough to keep the body from falling.

In the set position, sprinter should be less balanced, if the starter holds him for less than 2 seconds. When he is held for 2 seconds or longer, he will have assumed a more stable position, that is, with feet placed farther apart in the blocks. He must have such an unstable position in order to fall forward when he released his hands as support. His attention should be focused on sound, and any little noise would cause him to start immediately. He should concentrate, after hearing the sound on moving off the blocks as soon as possible. Thus, athlete's mental state should be such that the slightest noise will set him in motion. The sprinter must begin running as soon as the pistol is fired. He runs out of the blocks with the front leg driving hard.

At the set position, the hips are raised to a point slightly above the shoulders, so that as the runner leaves the blocks, he lifts his shoulders just above the hips. The force from the leg is then directed forward and only slightly upward. The idea of having the force from the legs go through the centre of the body and continue in a straight line to the finish tape points out to the sprinter the importance of being in a forward lean position at set, and of letting the legs continuously catch the body before it falls in its progress to the finish line, in a rhythmical, smooth motion.

To set an initial goal of a short distance only enables the runner to reach that particular point rapidly. Often the sprinter fails to maintain his pace from that point on because his body is too far forward. When practising sprint starting, the goal selected should be a distance of more than 20 yards. The eyes at set are focused on a point on the ground directly in front of the body, so that the head hangs down and is relaxed.

Some coaches contend that the sprinter should look at a point 3 to 20 yards down the track preparatory to starting. However, it is suggested that the raised head in the set position is tense. The runner should concentrate on taking the first step as rapidly as possible.

How to Leave the Blocks

Leaving the blocks properly is very essential for a good sprinter. At the sound of the gun, the slightly bent arm, opposite the stepping leg is quickly, but gently, thrust forward at shoulder level, but not as far as possible. The other arm is moved vigorously toward the rear so that the arms will move in opposition to the legs.

The first actual movement in starting is the cocking of the rear foot preparatory to taking a step. The front foot is then cocked just before the arms start their movement. The arms are actually hanging in front of the body when the first step is taken. This position keeps the body weight in front of the feet. The first step should be 18 to 30 inches from the starting line and slightly inward from a straight line down the track. The foot taking the first step should still be behind the weight centre line of the body and should barely clear the ground in moving forward.

Any lifting of the foot upward throws the body of the sprinter upward and prevents him from moving forward rapidly. The foot is pointed almost straight ahead as it strikes the ground. Excessive toeing inward or outward decreases foot and leg action. However, knee position is the real key to the sprinter's ability to direct his body in as straight a line as possible. The knee must be pointed in the direction of the run in order for the sprinter to move linearly. Slight toeing-out may not be as disadvantageous as once thought if the knee is pointed straight ahead. The head should be raised gently as the runner leaves the block so that he focuses on a spot 20 to 30 feet down the track ahead of him as he moves forward.

The sprinter should slowly come to a completely upright position. Each succeeding step should be longer until he reaches this up-right position. For most sprinters, this means that they have covered a distance of 10 to 15 yards before attaining their upright running position. If it were possible to have a higher effective starting position, full running stride could be achieved more rapidly. Short legged sprinters reach this position sooner than long-legged ones.

After leaving the blocks, the first few strides are fairly long, but not exaggerated in length. Short choppy steps should not be used. Reaction time off the blocks is not correlated with speed in the sprints. However, the better start each runner gets, the greater is his opportunity for running an ideal race. Probably, the two most important factors are that the sprinter gets a firm, fast start and attempts to maintain top speed as long as possible. Upon reach full running position, the sprinter should pull his hips under him and attempt to roll his hips as he runs, thereby increasing the length of each stride.

Since a sprinter reaches his maximum speed at approximately 65 yards from the start, or in approximately 6 seconds, the sprinter who is among the leaders at this point will win the race if he can come closer than the others to maintain this speed for the

remainder of the race. The use of proper arm and leg action is extremely important.

Going off the blocks, the sprinter should have strong arm action, with the movement to the front and rear made as fast as possible. As the sprinter reaches his full running position, the arm action should be rapid, but executed somewhat more in front the body. The movement of the bent arm to the front is rapid, but easy, so that the body will not react to the front arm movement with a backward motion.

The arms should move slightly in toward the middle of the body, but not much higher than shoulder level. This slightly inward swinging motion is necessary for smooth, relaxed action because of the anatomical connection of the arm with the rest of the body, and the way in which the chest muscles pull the arms forward and inward.

If the sprinter tends to tense his arms as he runs, it may be better to have him cut down the action of the arms, and swing them gently and easily in rhythm with the legs for balance purposes only. During the sprint, the hand should be slightly cupped with the thumb pushing against the forefinger.

Ability to relax the arm is an important factor in enabling the runner to secure entire body relaxation while running. Pushing the thumb against the forefinger helps prevent the arm from becoming tense. The legs, from the first step until slightly beyond the upright running position, are moved vigorously with a high knee lift. The high knee lift should be continued throughout a 100 yard sprint, but the foot action against the ground is not as vigorous when the sprinter uses longer strides.

There are deep holes in the ground after the first 5 or 6 strides, with the heel plainly visible. After that, the holes are much smaller, with the heel hitting very lightly and the marks barely visible. The movement of the leg to the rear is such that the foot goes somewhat higher than the knee. However, too much kick up in the rear appears to be unnecessary, does not add anything to the speed of movement, and results in loss of time. The knee lift in front should be high, almost even with the top of the hip. The leg and foot are extended forward so that a long stride is taken, with the foot striking the ground in pawing like action.

The sprinter should move his leg as fast as he can

and still take as long a stride as possible. However, leg speed should not be unduly sacrificed for a longer stride. The body lean forward at the start is extreme. This angle of lean gradually decreases until the vertical position is assumed as the runner reaches his upright running position.

While running, the leg of the rear foot, at the point of fullest extension, should be in a straight line with the back and the head. Some top runners have even been found to lean slightly backward during the latter position of the race. However, it is impossible to run forward without having the rear leg and foot, the motive force, exerting effort from the rear of the centre of the body weight. It is essential that the head be kept up during the run. Many beginning sprinters hold their heads down during the first few strides up at the start. This gives them a false illusion of gradually coming up to an erect running position. Unfortunately, they are working at a mechanical disadvantage and may lose because of their proper initial form. The running from throughout should be smooth and seemingly effortless. Galloping, rolling of the head and body from side to side, excessive movement of the hands and arms, and clenching of the teeth, which makes the neck and face muscles bulge, will decrease running speed. Feet and ankles move rapidly in a bounce-like action to increase the speed of leg and foot movement.

After the sprinter has come to an upright running position, he should run with a long unexaggerated stride varying according to his leg length and general build, probably somewhere between 6 and 9 feet. He should use a high lift, employ fast arm action, and keep a straight back.

Thus, it can be said that in order to run well, a sprinter must drive powerfully backwards by stretching legs to their fullest extent. This means that the arms must swing powerfully too and there should be a good split at the thighs from knee lift. The good sprinter appears to have no undue tension which comes from practice of the movements which enables him to time them properly without wasting energy. To tell whether a good start has been made, a run from the start of at least 50 to 60 metres is necessary and there is no such thing as a slow sprint start. A good sprinter does not roll his shoulders, run off line, and his spikes must leave a straight trail at about 2 inches or 3 inches either side of a line. Good sprinters run right through the tape and beyond the finishing line.

HURDLING

For the Hurdling it can said that it is a special form of sprinting. It is every fourth side in the sprinting hurdle

race which is different from the others, but the movements have to be performed in as near the same time as the sprinting stride as possible. Modern hurdling requires a tall athlete who has excellent hurdling technique combined with tremendous sprinting ability. This is particularly the case in the men's 110-metre hurdles, where the hurdles are 3 feet 6 inches tall.

However, in other hurdling events, the lower hurdles allow for a less exaggerated technique and greater variation in body size. Thus, it can be said that sprinting ability is must. The technique of hurdling has changed little over the past 30 years. In the 100/110-metre hurdles, elite athletes aim for three strides between each hurdle. They also attempt to spend as much time as possible on the ground sprinting and, conversely, as little time as possible in the air over each hurdle. This requires excellent hurdling technique, which can only be developed through a concentrated program of sprinting, hurdling and related flexibility exercises.

Thus, tall long-legged sprinters usually make the best hurdlers, but some athletes cannot adapt their running to the fixed stride pattern demanded and though they are good they never reach the top. Another quality a hurdler needs is suppleness or flexibility around the hip region. The would be hurdler must have the ability to withstand knocks and come back for more, for in order to cross the barriers effectively the hurdler must drive at them hard, from the very beginning. You cannot learn hurdling doing it slowly.

MIDDLE-DISTANCE RUNNING

The first recorded distance events, during the ancient Olympics, were run in stadiums at distances of seven to 24 stades (1400-4800 meters).

RUNNING

The steeplechase was developed in Great Britain in the 19th Century, evolving from cross country events where runners raced between towns, from one church steeple to another, facing natural obstacles along the way.

Although the marathon was inspired by the legend of the Athenian military courier Phidippides (or Philippides), who supposedly ran approximately 26 miles from the plains of Marathon to Athens in 490 B.C., the track and field event was first run at the 1896 Olympics. Those initial Olympics also included the 800- and 1500-meter runs. The 5000 and 10,000 were added in 1912 and the 3000-meter steeplechase in 1920.

The only distance event run by women when they began Olympic competition in 1928 was the 800. The 1500 was added in 1972, followed by the 3000 and the marathon in 1984 and the 10,000 in 1988. The 3000 was replaced by the 5000 in 1996.

Middle distance race is one in which full out effort can not be maintained throughout the race because the athlete has to replace the sugars from which he mainly derives his energy whilst he is still running. Events from the 800 metre race to the marathon are usually considered distance races.

Learning for all races from sprints to the longest distance requires improvement of the athlete's anaerobic and aerobic endurance. Aerobic endurance is controlled by the capacity of the heart, lungs and circulatory system to supply oxygen to the muscles for a long, sustained effort. Training for aerobic endurance is characterized by long runs at moderate speed. Anaerobic endurance is local muscular endurance, or the capacity of the muscular system to operate using stored fuel. Training for anaerobic endurance is characterized by all out effort over distances that are frequently shorter than the race distance.

RELAY RACES

Basically there are two types of relay, 4×100 metres and 4×400 metres, though combinations of distances like 880, 440, 220 sometimes feature on athletic programmes. There are also road and other long distance relays. All relays are team races where each member of the team runs a particular portion of the race.

In the 4×400 metre relay, only the first lap and the bend of the second lap are run in lanes. There are no change over zones, and a visual exchange is used rather than a blind pass, due to the fatigue and slower speed of the incoming runner. The outgoing runner turns to face the incoming runner and takes the baton out of the incoming runner's hand rather than being given the baton.

The aim of 4×100 metre relay is for runners to pass the baton while both sprint at top speed. A blind pass is used which means that the outgoing runner has no need to look back or turn and reach back for the baton. The

4×100 metre relay has three change over zones, each 20 metres in length, and prior to each change over zone is a 10 metre acceleration zone. The outgoing runner is allowed to accelerate within the 10 metre acceleration zone provided that the baton is exchanged in the 20 metre change over zone. In the kind of relay, elite athletes usually place a check mark 20 to 30 foot lengths from the start of the acceleration zone, and the outgoing runner begins accelerating when the incoming runner hits this check mark. A call from the incoming runner indicates when the outgoing runner must reach back for the baton.

Usually the exchange occurs approximately 5 metres prior to the end of the change over zone. With practice, the outgoing runner learns exactly where the exchange will occur and so is prepared for the call of the incoming runner.

An excellent 4×100 metre relay team sprints well and moves the baton at top speed. Good arm stretch must be used during the exchange so that each athlete runs the shortest possible distance during his or her leg of the relay.

STEEPLECHASE

This is an event which combines middle distance running, hurdling and water jumping, because of which requires training for the distance runner and the hurdling also. The rules of the event allow the athlete to jump on and off the water jump barrier and to use the same technique in clearing the steeplechase hurdles. The athlete is also permitted to vault over the barriers, although this method is seldom used because it is extremely inefficient.

The hurdles and the water jump barrier used in the steeplechase are solid, heavy barriers designed to support the weight of several athletes at the same time. The barriers are not designed to fall or to be knocked over in the manner that occurs in the 100/110-metre and 400-metre hurdles. Clearance of the water jump requires a technique similar to that used in jumping on and off steeplechase hurdles. The two types of obstacles differ in that the water jump not only has a barrier but also a 3.66 metre water pit, which the athlete must jump across or run through. The common practice is to jump up onto the 91.4 centimetre barrier with one leg and use the same leg to drive across the water. Occasionally, an athlete will jump from the barrier and totally clear the water, but most athletes land with 1 foot in the water and step out with the other.

An athlete who concentrates on steeplechase needs to be an excellent distance and cross country runner and a good hurdler and must be strong enough to perform efficiently over the water jump. One of the biggest difficulties that the steeplechaser will face is estimating takeoff positions for the hurdles and the water jump throughout the race relative to an increasing level of fatigue.

All steeplechaser jump on and off the water jump barrier. Some use the same technique on the hurdles, whereas other use a hurdle clearance similar to a 400 metre hurdler. Whatever the method, the athlete must cross the barriers as efficiently as possible and with minimum wastage of energy.

Thus some idea of various events included in the running must have been understood by this discussion, however detailed description of all the events have been made in the succeeding chapters alongwith their techniques and rules.

Important Information

Several additional comments about sprinting should be made. The great sprinters of the past learned to relax when they ran. One step in accomplishing relaxation is to let the swinging leg move partially unchecked until just before the vigorous thrust of the foot against the ground. Using the arms in such a manner that the forward motion is extremely easy and not under control of the muscles except is necessary for fast backward movement also helps in relaxing the runner. The back and the rear and front of the neck are among the areas apt to show most strain. To alleviate this strain, which often begins in the hands and arms, it is necessary for relaxation to begin in the hands and face.

Rolling the lip outward, or letting the lower jaw sag by opening the mouth, aids in relaxing the front of the neck and the face. The head and neck may be relaxed by keeping the head in line with the back. Lifting the head high at the start tends to tense the neck and back muscles. During the time the runner is accelerating, and especially while he is attempting to maintain his speed, it is important that he not overexert himself. This is not an easy skill to learn.

Every runner has a maximum rhythm of movement beyond which he cannot go. Trying to exceed this rhythm of movement slows and ties up the runner. Two breaths taken at the start of the sprint, and another as the runner gets set, enable the runner to hold his breath during part of a 100-yard race, usually for the duration of a 60-yard sprint. Taking one or two breaths at the beginning of a race also tends to relax the runner before he leaves the blocks.

At the 80-yard mark in the 100-yard sprint, one breath should be taken for a good supply of oxygen and to enable the runner to relax and run more easily at the finish. For distances beyond 100-yards, breathing normally seems to be the best technique, but the runner should taken one or more breaths at the start. Almost all runners hold their breath during an all-out effort, such as the last 25 yards of a long race. The sprinters who attempts to leap, jump, shrug or twist as he finishes a race is actually diminishing his speed with these extra motions. If any extra movement at the finish is necessary, it should be accomplished during the last stride.

Thus, the procedure a sprinter should follow to get success in the event has been explained above, but to follow the set procedure, one should have some qualities which can be developed by practising some specific drills which have been described below. The following drills play a large part in the improvement of sprinting technique. All drills benefit sprinter in one way or the other. These have been classified in various groups according to their objectives i.e. drills to improve coordination and drills to improve sprint endurance.

Improving the Coordination

An acceptable method for developing sprinting technique is to practice the correct elements slowly in a clockwork, formalized manner. Once beginners learn the correct actions and grasp the necessary rhythm, their speeds of movement are increased.

a. High-Knee Marching—Each participant marches forward slowly, forcefully driving the thigh of the leading leg up to horizontal. The arms are bent at 90 degrees at the elbow. The supporting leg extends fully up onto the toes as the participant lifts the opposing knee. For this drill, lift each thigh to horizontal, work your arms forward and backward, not across your body, and the push up vigorously onto your toes with each step.

b. High-Knee Skipping with Lower Leg Extension—This drill is quite strenuous, 3 to 4 short individual efforts, each followed by a rest, are sufficient to begin with for novices. The performer pretends to be skipping a rope. The thighs are raised to horizontal, and the lower leg is kicked out to an extended position. The performer looks straight ahead, holds the arms at 90 degrees at the elbows, and swings them forward and backward vigorously.

c. Seat Kicks—Each athlete moves slowly forward, kicking up the heels to the rear and attempting to hit the buttocks. This practice helps to establish the pattern of leg movement to the rear of the body and also stretches and loosens the quadriceps.

d. Counting Strides over a Selected Distance—The athlete sprints at medium to high speed over 20 to 25 metres, while you count the number of strides the athlete takes to run the distance. The athlete must try to maintain the same tempo throughout and maintain good technique without overstriding.

e. Sprint Arm Action—In this practice, the athlete concentrates on maintaining the angle of the arms at elbow together with a forward and backward swing that must be parallel to the direction of run. This is initially practised standing still, then walking, and thereafter jogging and sprinting.

Drills to Improve Leg Power

These activities are very demanding. Use them sparingly with beginners, and increase intensity and repetitions slowly. The recommended number of repetitions for beginners is 2 to 3 times with walking rests between each effort.

a. Distance Hopping—Swing your arms forward and upward as vigorously as possible to help gain distance. Drive powerfully with each jumping leg. Make each hop the same size. Do not hop for height, drive for distance. Try the hopping sequence from standing and then from a 2- to 3-step run-up.

b. Bounding for Distance—Lean forward slightly and jump long and low, not upward, keep the momentum going. Make each bounding stride about the same size. Drive forward and upward with your arms on each stride. Try the bounding strides from a standing start and then from a 2 to 3 step run-up.

c. Combinations of Hopping and Bounding over Low Obstacles—Bamboo canes set across cones are combined with mats to form a series of low obstacles. These are set in a sequence that forces the performer to strive for distance on each of 3 to 4 successive jumps. Mats cushion the landings. You make up the sequence of required hops and bounds.

d. Sprinting with Partner Resistance—Using a strap or belt, one athlete pulls another along like a horse and cart. The sprinter wears the strap or belt around the abdomen, with the partner holding the lines and providing a mobile but gentle resistance. The resistance should be sufficient to make the horse work as vigorously as possible, as though sprinting flat out.

Both horse and cart move forward 10 metres at a speed equivalent to a fast jog. A surface that provides sufficient traction will be necessary. Partners change roles after 2 to 3 repetitions.

e. Running, Bounding and Jumping Up Stairs—Running, bounding, hopping and jumping are performed up stairs, as the athlete's leg power increases, steeper stairs are used. This is a familiar activity for football players who run and bound up stadium steps as part of their training.

Introduce this activity on steps that are low and wide enough to allow plenty of room for each landing and takeoff. Initially, have students practice one type of jump at a time in order not to disrupt rhythm. Later, use combinations of all types of jumps. Experienced athletes may also bound down shallow stairs using a controlled double leg take-off and double-leg landing.

Drill to Improve Sprint Endurance

a. Continuous Relays—Form a team of 9 members. Each team member runs 50 metres on a 400-metre track. First player runs 50 metres then passes the baton to or tags second player for the next round of exchange. Ninth player moves into first player's position to receive the tag from eight number player.

b. Rolling Sprints—Teams of four jog or run slowly around the track. At the signal, fourth player sprints to the front of the team. On the next signal, third player sprints to the front and so on.

Reducing the time between signals and increasing the size of teams will increase the intensity. One full lap of a 400-metre track is adequate for beginners.

c. Interval Sprints—Participants sprint the curve and jog or walk the straightaway on a 400-metre track, or they sprint 50 metres and jog or walk 200 to 300 metres. They repeat the interval 3 to 4 times. The length and type of rest depends on the fitness and performance ability of the athlete. The pulse rate provides a good measure, if the pulse falls below 120 beats per minute at the end of the rest, the next repetition can begin. If the pulse stays above 120, the intensity of training is too high and should be reduced.

Training Program

Certain training and conditioning principles are recommended for the sprinter which are:

i. most endurance running should be done in early season;

ii. fast starting with a gun should be practised at least once a week throughout the season;

iii. an all-out effort for short distances should be made at every practice session;

iv. movies of each runner should be taken and analysed early in the season;

v. starts and short runs should be scheduled at the first part of each practice session;

vi. easy workouts in late season are often the most beneficial for the competitive performer;

vii. confidence can be built by having the sprinter win some races.

The sprinter does not need much equipment in order to perform well in his event. While his clothing must not fit snugly and bind his body or limbs, it should not be so loose that it flaps as he runs. The legs of the running trunks should be loose enough to allow free motion of the runner's leg. His shoes should be snug and should adhere closely to the feet. Shoes with some spikes placed near the front of the sole have the best leverage position.

For hard surface tracks, the short spikes are best, including indoor board tracks, long spikes are best for outdoor competition. Some warm up for the sprinter is necessary. It appears that physiological effects similar to those resulting from a warm up can be secured through excitement, heat, hypnosis, and other means. A runner who is so weak from excitement that he does not feel like running up and down the track prior to a race probably needs very little warming up, and that mostly for relaxation purposes.

The main value in the warm-up for speed events is that the runner gets a feel of the track and gains confidence in his own ability as he sees that he can run and is able to move with very little effort. On a cold day, it is better for a sprinter to keep warm in his sweat suit near a furnace or heater than to go out on the track for a lengthy warm-up session. He should be excited enough about the race that only a minimum of time is spent on the track, to help him prepare for the race.

Safety Suggestions for Sprinters

Because of their simplicity, sprinting events require fewer safety regulations than throwing or jumping events. However, you should consider several points. Sprinting is a highly explosive event, and it is essential that the sprinter warm up thoroughly prior to all training sessions and competitions, this reduces the likelihood of muscle tears and pulls.

The warm up should begin with light, easy running and flexibility exercises. Intensity is increased with fast striding, short sprints, and practice starts. The athlete must be particularly careful with some of the special activities used for developing sprinting technique, such as high-knee running and high-knee skipping, which can produce hamstring pulls and other muscle injuries unless preceded by a careful warm-up. This problem can affect even a well-conditioned athlete who fails to warm up adequately.

Of modern sprinting, weight training has become an important element, but it must always be coupled with stretching and flexibility exercises specifically chosen to complement sprinting. Overuse of weights can be detrimental to sprinting, and weight lifting should always be practised as a secondary form of training. In hot weather, athletes frequently take off their spikes and run on the infield barefoot, so it is essential that spikes and spike pins are stored properly.

Strictly control starting pistols and their ammunition, lock them in a safe place when they are not in use. In no circumstance leave a loaded starting pistol unattended. Starting pistol ammunition is designed specifically for track competitions, and it should not be used for any other purposes. The loss of starting pistols must be immediately reported to the appropriate authorities. An excellent substitute for a starting pistol is a pair of starting clappers. This is made of two boards hinged at the base, with half of a black and white disk attacked to each board. The crack of the boards when they are brought together gives an acoustical signal that starts the athletes. The black and white halves of the disk when brought together give a visual signal for starting stopwatches.

2

SKILLS AND TECHNIQUES OF RUNNING

MIDDLE DISTANCE RUNNING

RUNNING

A middle distance race is one in which full out effort cannot be maintained throughout the race, because the athlete has to replace the sugars from which he mainly derives his energy whilst he is still running. Those who can do this most efficiently whilst running the fastest pace are the best runners.

To the layman, distance running must appear to be the least complicated form of track and field athletics. There is no aerodynamic equipment necessary, as in the throwing events; no resorting to clandestine use of anabolic steroids in order to develop a grotesque, bulky body; no preoccupation with the technique practice as in the jumps events. In fact, it might seem that, all a distance runner needs to do to improve is simply run, run and run more. This is not the reality. Today, running event has become very important and widely popular event in the world and now its modern face is very complicated for which the runner has to learn various skills.

Middle distance races include the 800-metre, 1500-metre and mile races. Long distance races include the 3000 metre steeplechase, 5000-metre, 10,000-metre, and marathon races.

Basically, athlete performing distance running has to distribute his energy efficiently and completely over a particular distance. Endurance is considered an important and primary factor in such a kind of running. Today, this event has gained worldwide popularity and standard of performance of runners has improved considerably.

Following are some features of the technique of

running, which help the runner to perform well:

i. General movement of the body and the arms limited to essentials;

ii. Very little up and down movement of the body;

iii. Economical and smooth striding;

iv. A mental attitude which enables the runner to keep going even when fatigue pains are gripping him. Breaking the pain barrier;

v. Even paced rhythm to the striding. All out effort at the end;

vi. Head kept still; eyes fixed on the track; and

vii. Moderated leg drive in line with the direction of running. No wasted movements.

Technique

Distance runner's technique consists of upright body position, however, a little slight forward lean may occur. The stride length in longer distance is shorter while in shorter distance it is moderate to long. While increasing speed, runner can reduce the length of the stride. Depending on distance and phase of the race, he can lift the knee and leg drive. He should raise his knee in sprinting phases while keep the arm at the same level.

Learn Distance Running Step-By-Step

For the coach who needs to build up athletes gradually to a point at which they can be given individual schedules, it is useful to get them involved with enjoyable with groups of other people of the same age or ability. To begin with, the athlete will wish to know how he compares with others, so a short race over a cross-country course would be a useful guide.

Based on the ages of the athletes, a distance of perhaps approximately 3000m could be selected.

Races at Initial Level

The group set off all together from a point which ensures a sufficiently long distance to the first stage, gap in a hedge, or other funnelling that could result in a bunching-up of the athletes. On reaching the finish, each athlete is timed to the nearest second, and a ranking list is prepared showing the name of the athlete, his time and by what amount of time he beats the next runner. An additional column can be prepared which shows in reverse order by how many minutes or seconds the last runner was behind each runner.

Ringing the Changes

Another form of running training that can be adopted is to take the final column of race, and start a race with Runner (I) setting off alone; his objective is not to be overtaken. 35 seconds later Runner (V) sets off with the same objective and also attempts to overtake Runner (VI). 50 seconds later Runner (IV) sets off and so on until, 1 min. 50 secs after Runner (VI) started, Runner (I) leaves, hoping to beat his previous best time for the course and overtake as many athletes as possible in route.

One can get the following important information through this race:

- Which athletes beat their previous best time;

- Who had the fastest time for the course;

- How many athletes overtook others during the race.

Such changes of runs lend interest, provide incentive for greater effort, and often increase the enjoyment. Further modes of training in the early stages can include pairing off the runners.

The objective of such a race would be that the combined times of each pair would be recorded, and those obtaining the lowest time would win.

Hares and Hounds and Paper Chase

Hares and Hounds, were one or two athletes set off over a known course a minute or so before the remainder, who attempted to catch him before he returned back to the starting place. In countries, where the litter laws permit it, an interesting form of competition is for two runners to set off with bags of small pieces of paper on their backs. Their course is a secret, and they are given one or two minutes' start. The pursuers see the direction in which the athletes have gone, but once out of sight, they can change direction, provided they leave a trail of chalk, paper, etc., showing where they have gone.

The main objective is to catch the trail-leavers before they return back to the starting point. Related to this type of activity is orienteering, a sport which involves participants with maps and compasses covering a predetermined route, visiting a number of check-points, and attempting to complete the course as quickly as they can.

Track Practices

Having provided a base of fitness through increasing amounts of enjoyable running, the coach should begin to organise other practices based at the track. In the first instance, athletes can be required to carry out simple repetition runs , then pair-running system.

Pair-running or parrlauf is an interesting form of distance, say eight laps of the track, is first decided upon. The athletes are divided into pairs and each pair decides how to divide the race between them; only one of the athletes needs to be running at any one time. This can be done in the following ways:

a. Athlete (i) can run the first two laps, then Athlete (ii) two laps, then Athlete (i) two laps, concluding with Athlete (ii) two laps;

b. Athlete (i) can run the first four laps and Athlete (ii) the last four;

c. They can run alternate laps;

d. Athlete (i) can run 200m and touch Athlete (ii), who runs the next 200m. In the meantime, Athlete (i) cuts across the centre grass area of the track to his original starting point where Athlete (ii) hands over the race to him. Athlete (ii) also cuts across the track ready to take over at his own 200m point.

e. If Athlete (i) is a better athlete then Athlete (ii) it may be decided to allocate over half of the running to Athlete (i).

Having begun to mix track work with cross-country practices, the coach will now be able to observe which athletes are ready to be given individual training programmes.

Training Tactics

Group of Distance Race includes the events from 800-metre race. Beginning runners can considered it a long sprint. Runner is expected to improve his anaerobic and aerobic endurance, for which he can get assistance from a coach.

Aerobic endurance of a runner depends on the capability of runner's heart, lungs and circulatory system to supply oxygen for a longer period of time, while anaerobic endurance depends on the capability of muscular system to operation using stored fuel. For aerobic endurance, runner should run over long distances at different speeds, whereas for anaerobic endurance, runner should run over considerable shorter distances than race distance. The performance of a runner depends basically on runner's anaerobic capacity. With increase in demand, pressure on anaerobic endurance decreases and shifts to aerobic endurance.

However, it does not imply that runner is required to perform only aerobic training, instead anaerobic training is also necessary. Distance runner should be capable of maintaining fast speed and sprint all the time. Because of this reason, training of distance runner should be designed in such a manner, that it covers not only aerobic endurance but also anaerobic endurance.

Training session of beginning runners of long distance races should commence in off-season and work till competitive season. In the initial stage of his training schedule, he should be learning simple and slow runs, however at later stage, however at later stage he can learn high speed runs.

In the following manner training schedule of a beginning runner should design:

a. In the beginning, runner should be taught aerobic endurance;

b. Once runner has properly learnt aerobic endurance, he should then attempt some sort of anaerobic endurance exercises also;

c. He should include in his training only those exercises which specifically stress on endurance and is important from point of view of the event. With increase in distance, stress on anaerobic endurance decreases.

Training

Middle distance running cannot be compared with a technique event such as pole vaulting or high jumping and once an athlete can run in an economical style the bulk of his or her time should be spent on body conditioning. This means, improving the ability of the body to recover quickly not only after, but during exercise. Improvement in this comes quickly at first but gradually, the amount of improvement is less and there comes a time when it could be a question of months or a whole season, not days and weeks, before any real improvement in performance in seen.

To run a middle distance race well, requires practice over a long period, and in this event, there are always people to train with, as middle distance running is very popular.

Technique of Training

As training is very important for this event, athlete should understand the manner in which he should get the training:

a. It should be regular;

b. It should be interesting and he should vary his work;

c. It should increase in difficulty as time goes on.

d. It should be kept up over a period of months.

e. It should be for a specific object.

f. It should include competition; and

g. Different types of training for different effects are required, e.g., strength, stamina, speed. Alternate the days on which these are done.

Strength, stamina and speed are inter-related and one effects the other. It is often a question of emphasis.

Safety Suggestions

Now-a-days, distance running has become a very popular event throughout the world. The reason for this fact can be considered that to practice this event, any kind of equipment is not required, and it can be practised and learnt anywhere. However, this event is quite risky for which runner should keep in his mind some safety factors in his mind. While planning cross-country, fartlek and jogging trails, runner should carefully considered these factors. Runner should plot the course in such a manner that it does not cross other traffic lanes. Help of police should be taken if race is to be performed on the road. All the things which can cause the runners collide, should be removed.

While running on roads, runner should keep his head straight and wear easy to see colours. During training, he should be very careful at intersections and run with partners. Runners should not run alone on lonely trails.

In training schedules as well as in competitions, runner should take in his mind the number of participants involved, type of weather and length of the run. Weather conditions play a very important part in competitions, as in hot weather runner has to take fluid rapidly, while in cold weather he has to wear warm clothes.

There is no particular criterion of a runner's clothing, however, he should switch to such a dress in which he can run comfortably. A runner's performance not only depends on his dressing, but also on his shoes, thus he should be very careful in selecting his shoes. He should opt for such shoes, in which he feels comfortable and safety.

Training schedule of a runner should not include only heavy running, but to give comfort to him, a warm-up session should be there in it. After running for long distance continuously, runner becomes tired and loses his energy and capacity, for which he should be provided relaxation time. Thus, such drills should be a part of his training schedule, which provides him relaxation. The kinds and duration of drills included in a warm-up session should be decided by the coach. The basic aim of warm-up session should be to provide psychological as well as physiological relaxation to the runner.

In the initial stage of training, the coach should not impose heavy drills and heavy work on the athlete by which he loses the interest in the event. Thus, coach should keep in his mind that he should keep the interest of the athlete aroused in the event.

Significance of Style in Distance Running

An uneconomical technique of running must be

cured by the coach, but it is stressed that there is no ideal method of running. Emil Zatopek adopted a head and shoulder roll with tongue hanging out and an agonised facial expression; Arthur Wint had a massive stride length and a most relaxed look about him; Bruce Tulloh shuffled along in bare feet with arms bunched tightly across his body.

Basically, the most important criterion is comfort. If an athlete's natural style is mechanically inefficient, causing him to expend extra energy, then the coach will modify the style; otherwise, there need be no interference.

Breathing should be through the mouth and nose, there should be no attempt to lengthen the stride, and there should be a minimum of tension especially in the face and neck muscles. Towards the end of a race, the style will necessarily change, the knees coming through higher and the arms driving more.

It is true that there is an ideal form of style for each event, however, this varies from athlete to athlete. A runner can choose his own style in which he can perform comfortably. With age and experience style of a runner changes, however, it takes a considerable amount of time. With changes in ability of a runner to run, his style also gets changed. Even, styles of a runner for different distance run can vary, i.e., a runner will run differently in half-mile, differently in a mile and differently in two-mile distance run.

There is not any particular criterion with which a proper style can be judged, however one can evaluate his style with respect to the following factors:

i. Body angle;
ii. Arm swing;
iii. Foot placement;
iv. Length of stride;
v. Rear-leg lift; and
vi. Over-all action.

Body angle

Generally, with speed, body of the runner begins to lean forward. All human movement is a process of falling with balance, a constant loss and recovery of balance.

Because of this, one cannot prevent the increased angle of speed running. Runner usually faces with the problem of keeping the body straight. For this, he should keep his eyes properly on the ground. Body will come in proper angle if runner places his eyes on the ground ahead and head properly on the ground. This point on which runner will focus his eyes depends on the style of runner and the pace with which he runs.

Arm swing

While running, runner should keep his arms relaxed. The main considerations for coaches should be balance and rhythm. With speed, arm movement of the runner will increase and become more energetic. Not at any speed, runner should lost the relaxation and smoothness of his arms.

For proper arm movement, a coach can give the following instructions to the runners:

a. Drop the hands to side and relax them completely;

b. Place the thumbs and forefingers together;

c. Keeping the hands relaxed, lift the hands to a level equal or below the hips;

d. As arms of a doll might swing on a pin through the shoulders, let the arms swing from the shoulder girdle, do not drive them and let them go of their own weight and inertia and relax;

e. Keep the angle of the forearm with the upper arm same throughout and do not swing the hands high or near the face instead, keep them relaxed and low.

Once a runner has successfully brought his arms

in proper swinging position, he is not required to work on them more. He should drop them and shake them if they have become heavy and tired while running.

For this, in the beginning, runner should perform easy and simple arm action and then perform some exercises of arms.

Foot placement

Foot placement of a runner varies according to the style of running and speed and distance of run. Better utilisation of effort is the primary consideration, but where speed is increasingly important, length and springiness of stride should be carefully coached and practised. At all three distances—the 880, the mile, and the two-mile, the landing should be made first on the ball of the foot.

Runner should drop the weight lightly on the heel in case of 880, while in the two-mile a greater concern for economy will allow a somewhat greater process of settling and relaxing to occur before bouncing back to the ball and toes. Body weight of the runner will shift forward in faster run.

Thus, foot placement of a runner will keep on changing with change in distance of run. This is a natural phenomena and runner himself has to decide, in which foot step style he can perform with ease and comfort.

Length of stride

These days, many runners are using high-toed, bouncing and long-striding action of sprinters. To run over one-half mile, runner has to correct this wasteful stride. For this purpose, runner can make use of Cross-Country work and Fartlet.

Matter of length of stride is very important and with increase in distance of race, stride will decrease. Thus, there establishes an inverse relationship between speed of race and length of stride.

Rear-leg lift

Now-a-days it is suggested to the runners that lift of rear lower is of no use, thus importance is being placed on full forward-reaching stride and knee lift. Runner should swing rear foot upward and backward as soon as the leg starts forward, by this, lower leg and heel swings near the upper biceps. This decreases the weight arm of the leg level and length of pendulum

Lower leg falls easily as soon as upper leg swings forward. To permit the foot to clear the ground, knee swings in forward and upward direction. Runner should not attempt to length the stride, no forward reaching or pointing of toes because this results in tension and waste of energy. This rear-leg lift is not a deliberate backward throw a kick, whereas, it is a relaxed follow-through and follow-up of push of the rear foot from the ground.

Generally, runner can perform this himself, however, he can get the help of a coach. Runner should specifically concentrate on relaxation, naturalness, and rhythm of the total action.

The over-all action

There is not any particular criterion for over-all action, only it should be efficient, smooth and relaxed.

Runner should swing his arms and legs in a rhythm and smoothly. Basically, all the parts of the body should be in a balanced position and in a line.

Technique of Setting the Speed

Runner has to deal with the problem of facing the speed in the third phase of the race, when he becomes tired and heavy. At this time, speed of every runner falls.

It is generally found that runners in the beginning stage run very fast but over time, their speed and pace decreases and they remain behind in the race. A runner should avoid this situation and attempt to make his speed uniform throughout the race. For this, the runner should have considerable physical efficiency, relaxation and a rhythm. It is a very difficult thing to achieve for a runner, but he has to bring himself in such a state. For this, he requires long hours of practice and concentration. Runner should not run faster than his ability to discourage his opponent, as it is prove harmful and bad for himself.

In the beginning, runner can run with his full ability, but after reaching beyond all the runners he should attempt to bring his pace in a rhythm and should run smoothly. To keep himself far from the feeling of fatiguelessness, runner should think about his opponent's style, their pace and such things. Runners should not look around the track, rather they should run keeping their head and body straight. They should not attempt to watch the position of their opponents.

Runner should sprint at least two strides beyond the finish line. Just before the finish line, he should relax for a little time. To exert a pressure on his opponents, runner should keep himself always alert and capable to take decisions in different situations, for this he an make a plan in advance. Correct speed is important in the 880, for lap times come too late in the race to permit a satisfactory adjustment of mistakes.

Useful Kinds of Training

Basically, two kinds of training a runner should get:

i. Aerobic Training; and

ii. Anaerobic Training.

Aerobic Training

This type of training improves a runner's endurance or stamina by increasing the ability to take in and utilize oxygen, is accomplished through runs of 3 to 10 miles or longer at different speeds.

An easy tempo involves relaxed recovery running a brisk temp involves running at steady state or oxygen balance; and a hard tempo involves running beyond steady state but not all-out. Early training should include only easy and brisk tempo runs for several weeks; later, hard-tempo runs with hills may be alternated with easier runs.

Anaerobic Training

This type of training improves the body's ability to run while under oxygen debt is best developed through intermitten or interval-type training. Interval training consists of running a number of short distances at a given pace, interspersed by 1 to 5 minutes of rest or jogging fixed distances. Interval training is used basically to develop race rhythm and sharpening speed.

All kinds of valuable training have been discussed in detail below:

Interval Training

Some group of athletes of yesteryear and the present day have preferred this systematic form of training. In this training, the objective is to adapt the heart to the stress of running in endurance events. When training over distances in the region of 100, 200 and 400m, it has been found that middle-distance runners' hearts become stronger and pump blood around the muscles in greater volume, provided they run the chosen distance fast and take a pause of about 45 to 90 seconds before they run the next repetition.

It is proved in the researches, that after a fast run of 200m the heart fills rapidly with blood. If the athlete jogs slowly for about 45 seconds, the amount of blood arriving at the heart is decreased. Athlete should then repeat the procedure many times, with intervals of sprinting followed by intervals of slow jogging, the cavities of the heart increase in size and adapt themselves to receive more blood, thus providing more fresh blood to be supplied throughout the body.

During a training session, this system can gradually lose its effect. This has been shown to occur when an athlete's heart rate is over 180 beats per minute. Coaches therefore tend to limit their athletes' sprints to the period when the heart-rate is between 120 and 150 beats per minute, the rest between each run allowing the heart-rate to drop to that range.

Following are the disadvantages of this method:

i. It makes an athlete too dependent on stop-watch performance;

ii. It is boring; and

iii. The volume of blood pumped out of the heart at each stroke is only one consideration, the number of strokes per minute also being important.

Long Distance as Training

It is not only athletes of the distant past who have used the long distance method for the bulk of their training, many new athletes are also using this method. Some athletes who believe in the value of this system will train well over 100 miles in total each week, and will include runs of 20 miles or more in at- least one day. Some athletes doing this kind of training are 800 meters runners. But athletes should not rely solely on this method, for though it has an advantageous effect on the circulo-respiratory system and therefore provides a good basis for other types of training, actual racing consists of changes of pace including fast bursts as well as the slower pace, and so the heart needs to be accustomed to a variety of changes during training.

Resistance Running

Athlete should use this running when he is making it harder and difficult for himself to run, like, running on hills, running in boots, or in sand or soft ground. Whether the hills are mud, snow, sand or coal seems not to matter, provided that the athletes are required to run them up fast, using their arms vigorously, and repeat the runs often.

Other kinds of this training include harness-running, running in heavy boots, running with sacks of sand on the back and running with weighted belts. Wearing a weighted waistcoat, or running towing a roller and similar activities which build up strength and endurance come in this group.

Whenever a coach employs these methods, he should consider the objective, and whether the same effect could be obtained in another way. Sometimes coaches tend to become slaves to one method which has value only at limited periods during a year.

Fartlek

It places the onus on the athlete to decide when to place the effort and is best carried out over a country course which provides an interesting array of hills, fast stretches and rough ground. It involves running over different types of country at different and changing speeds. The name means speed play. The effectiveness of this training in building up general stamina is related to the amount and type of work put in.

Though an experienced athlete will be able to push himself to include more fast running stretches than slower ones, less experienced athletes might need direction. A coach could accompany his athletes, giving directions.

This drill is interesting to do because there is a variety of terrain and change of pace and emphasis which can fulfil the athlete's needs. A typical course might include speed running on the flat road or on the grass, jogging, through the woods, dodging quickly in and out of trees, uphill running, fast walking, a short race, say between two lamp posts on the road section or from the bottom to the top of a hillock and back, running through sand, soft soil or over plough land, along a path across parkland and on the track.

Cross Country Running

It is the running over the country without any particular plan of training in view. It is not necessarily racing though this need not be ruled out. It is good for early season built up of strength and stamina.

Tempo Running

In addition to efficient hearts and lungs, athletes must also consider the fatigue in the arms, shoulders and leg muscles that is evident at the end of race. One form of training that prepares athletes for this is where the coach requires them to do very fast runs between which there is a very short rest.

Thus the athlete is expected to perform with great amounts of lactic acid in the muscle incurring what is known as oxygen debt. Eventually, the athlete manages to cope with his anaerobic activity and the pain of the fatigue. This is an arduous form of training even for experienced athletes and should not constitute the sole method of training.

Timed Running

It involves the use of measured periods of fast running interspersed with rest periods during which the runner jogs or even rests completely. The method of altering the effects of timed or controlled training is by altering any of the following:

a. Speed of the fast running;
b. Length and speed of the resting period;
c. The number of periods done; and
d. The length of fast part.

By having a short resting section, the body learns to readjust itself more quickly. The resting periods are shorter between short fast runs and gradually lengthen as the runs get longer, but a three to four minutes jog is about the maximum rest for effective work.

The length of the fast running period in middle distance training is nearly always less than the length of the actual race distance, but it is run at a faster pace. In working out speeds for use in any running practice, the plan should be to run shorter distances at faster than race speed, and to do many short distances, which, when added together, would make more than the race distance.

Paarlauf

This running includes in teams of two. Each team runs one man at a time in rely fashion to see how much ground can be covered in a fixed time and runners decide on their speeds and distances. This is a form of Timed Running.

Training Schedule

Athlete should decide himself that what type of training he wants to emphasise and then he should work out a weekly schedule on its basis.

Important: Before any training session, athlete should warm up wearing appropriate clothing, e.g., track-suit, sweater, etc. This might take from 10 to 20 minutes depending on the climatic conditions.

Warming Up Schedule

As mentioned above, before going through any training session, athlete should warm up. He can make his warming up schedule in the following manner:

i. He should jog slowly round 440 yd track, taking about 1¾ minutes and begin the second lap slowly and increase the speed in the last 100 yds, so that he can sprint home. This he should do for 4 minutes.

ii. For 2 minutes, he should do a series of bending, stretching and loosening exercises and perform one or two runs in spikes, gradually accelerating to a sprint at about 50 yds, then go full out for 20 yds and jog back.

iii. For 5 minutes, he should practice two or three 20 yd sprint starts; and at last

iv. He should jog around for at least until at least 2 minutes breath is recovered.

Allowing time for clothing changes, warming up takes about 15 minutes.

STEEPLECHASE

Learn Steeplechase Step-by-Step

i. The intending steeplechaser needs to be soundly fit, and have had his endurance developed over a long period of time by the particles.

ii. The intending steeplechaser needs to have

developed a good hurdling technique over a 3ft., high barrier. This will have been acquired over a period of time in practices.

iii. Additional practice must be given for the water jump technique. This will be done first of all by getting the athlete to run, step on a steeplechase hurdle, and continue running a short distance.

Effort will be applied on top of the hurdle so that the athlete will be driving forward as far away from the hurdle as possible.

iv. Having acquired proficiency at driving off a steeplechase hurdle, the next stage is to carry out the same practice at the water jump hurdle, but with no water in the water jump; at the learning stage, the athlete will not be driving sufficiently far off the hurdle;

v. The final beginner stage is the use of a check-mark a short distance before the water jump, so that the athlete can arrange his feet in such a way that he can be running fast at the water jump hurdle. Then comes the point at which the athlete must be able to run laps, in each of which, hurdles and a water jump are included.

A steeplechase well run is a fine event to watch, but there are a lot of duds in the game now-a-days who, because they will not trouble to learn to take the obstacles properly, spoil the race from the spectator's point of view. In the very early days of athletic meetings, steeplechase were undoubtedly numerous and most popular with the public. The inclusion of such an event in those days was, however, almost inevitable, since early sports meetings very often took the form of a point to point across country for a wager; one or two sprints and jumps being thrown in to keep the spectators amused with the big men of the occasion were racing out and home across country.

However, when athletics reached the cinder path stage, the steeplechase was only included at sports meetings, because the runners inevitably fell at the water jump, arousing a laugh from the on-lookers. Lather on paper-chasing came into vogue as a serious sport, and then the steeplechase recovered its popularity with sports promoters.

From the days of revival of interest in this event, wide water-jumps and cruelly prickly bramble-fences began to disappear. The distance, moreover, became more or less standardised at from three-quarters of a mile to two miles.

To be a good steeplechaser, one must be a good distance runner, capable of sound judgment of pace and race tactics, and also a good hurdler. Steeplechaser should learn to surmount all the obstacles economically. Beginners has seen tackle the obstacles in all sorts of ways. Many increase the pace as they approach the hedge in front of the water and use up much strength in a great spring which carries them to the far edge of the river, but never quite over it. Others have been observed climbing laboriously to the top of the hedge, thereby losing much valuable time, in the hope that they will be able to make a standing jump which will carry them right over the water, but it seldom does; and in any case the amount of energy expended is out of all proportion to the result attained.

On the other hand, experts lope easily over the hedge

and drop lightly into the water with one foot a little in advance of the other, and the landing so planned that they can stride through the stream straight on to the dry land and away without checking the speed or breaking the rhythm of the run more than is absolute needed.

For a three-quarter mile steeplechase the training on the flat needs to be at about two miles and for a two miles race the steeplechaser should train himself, or be trained to accomplish good time on the flat at four miles. In either case, the greatest care and the most painstaking practice should ensure eleverness in negotiating the obstacles with the least possible expenditure of energy.

Fundamental Principles of Steeplechase

For every athlete who want to be a steeplechaser, it is necessary to learn the skill of crossing of obstacles. Steeplechasers are always trying to get their time for the race as near as they can to their flat race time for the distance. Crossing the obstacles adds on the seconds.

In the beginning, athlete may find himself vaulting some of the hurdles and since they are heavy and solid and firm and its a tiring race, this is a possibility, but a good steeplechasers hurdle.

Another problem generally faced by the athlete is to cross to perform the water jump, where he has to put his foot on the hurdle to drive himself over. Following guidelines should be kept by the athlete while performing this event:

i. To be moving a little faster as he comes to the hurdle which is in front of the jump. The top is 5 in. wide.

ii. To have a check mark well back so that athlete can come on confidently and hit his take-off point with the same foot each time;

iii. To keep low going over the hurdle, athlete should roll over the foot, but not need to take too much weight on it;

iv. To drive onwards rather than upwards;

v. To land so that the athlete is moving forwards;

vi. To bring the rear leg through and up ready to go into the next stride;

vii. Only enough energy to get over is required by the athlete. He should not waste it by going too hard at it and too high of it.

Prior to actually using the water jump, athlete should make use of the other hurdles and a mark on the track or grass 12 feet from it to simulate the far edge of the water.

Athlete should run at this hurdle, where he should put his foot up on the rail and push off landing on his other foot about 10 feet away and then run on. In this manner, he can:

a. Practise pushing off and keeping low;

b. Practise the smooth transition from landing into the next stride;

c. Get some idea of where his check mark will come;

d. Decide on the take-off foot.

After this attempt, athlete can try the actual water jump but he should sure himself that landing area is safe.

Training

During the winter, steeplechasers should be trained with a maximum of cross-country racing, middle-distance running and occasional hurdling. During the summer, steeplechasers should continue a middle-distance runner's programme, adding hurdling and water jump techniques on one or two days, dependent upon the runner's level of skill.

RELAY RACES

There are two types of relays:

a. Sprint relays, sprint medley; and

b. Distance relays and distance medley.

Four runners compete for a team, each running an equal distance, and pass a baton to the next runner. The baton must be exchanged within a 20-metre exchange zone.

4×100 Metres Relay

Throughout the world there is a mis-taken belief that all that is required to create a successful relay team is to put together the first four athletes from country's 100 metres championships and spend a small amount of time on baton practice. Some team selectors make a gesture to signify their greater understanding by including one or two 200 metres runners. But generally, not enough time is spent considering what the needs are for each particular leg of the relay.

Shuttle Relays

Where 400m track are not available, much

enjoyment, effort and skill may be forthcoming from shuttle relays. These can be organised in the gymnasium or on playing fields and are not confined to one team per lane necessarily, because they could be run without the use of lanes, neither are they restricted to only four athletes per team.

Shuttle relay organisation involves lining up the team side by side, one half of each team behind a line facing the other half of each team some distance away. On the signal from the coach, Runner I should run to touch the outstretched hand of Runner II, who must not commence till Runner I has crossed the predetermined line. Runner II then runs to touch Runner III and so on.

If a baton is used, it reduces the tendency to cheat and introduces an additional skill. Such relays could be introduced as warm-up at school levels and could include mixed teams of men and women specialising in such different events as shot-put, high-jump and hurdles etc.

Baton Passing

There are basically two methods to exchange the baton, namely, Visual Pass and Blind Pass.

i. Visual Pass: The visual pass is used in all distance relays. It enables the outgoing runner to judge the speed and fatigue of the incoming runner.

In this exchange, the outgoing runner, who is turned towards the inside of the track facing the pole lane, stands on the right side of the lane and receives the baton in the left hand, palm up, from the incoming runner's right hand. Upon receiving the baton, the outgoing runner should always immediately transfer the baton to the right hand.

ii. Blind Pass: The blind pass is used in sprint relays. In this exchange, the outgoing runner stands in a good sprint position at the back of the 10-metre fly zone located beyond the 20-metre zone. The runner stands on the left side of the lane, if the baton is to be received in the right hand, and the right side of the lane when the baton is to be received in the left hand. When the incoming runner hits a predetermined mark on the track, called the go mark, the outgoing runner leaves, concentrating on good sprinting action. This go mark may vary by 5 to 8 meters and is established by a trial and error method. The baton is exchanged at a given point in the zone, preferably in the last 10 meters of the 20-metre passing zone, without the receiver looking back. The exchange is made by the incoming runner by extending the baton forward as far as possible and placing the baton downward into the receiver's opposite hand, which has been extended backward, palm up.

In the 400-metre relay, it is best to handoff; first exchange from right to left, second exchange from left to right and third exchange from right to left, to make it possible for curve runners to be on the inside of the running lane.

a. Athlete must first be introduced to it by working in twos at walking pace. The athlete at the back places the baton in the desired fashion into the hand of the athlete in the front, then walks briskly to the front to receive the baton from his partner. This continuous passing has the added objective of giving practice at receiving in both hands.

b. The next is to complete the passing routine at a jog. Here the additional difficulties of keeping the receiving arm still, while jogging and of handing over the baton to a possibly moving target are introduced.

c. The speed of the exchange practice can be increased with all the athletes having practice of receiving and passing the baton using alternately left and right hands. These practices enable athletes to discover whether they are better in receiving or passing a baton, and which of their hands is the most adept at this skill.

d. As soon as the baton passing has been practised at speed, it must be remembered that the baton must also be received within a limited area, the take-over zone of 20m.

To ensure that this is carried out accurately, check marks need to be used. These are the marks placed on the track; when the mark is reached by the incoming runner, the outgoing runner knows that he must start running.

e. Check mark distances are calculated after much trial and error. The most conveniently accurate method of measuring them is for the outgoing runner to measure from the beginning of the take-over zone in foot lengths towards the athlete who is going to pass to him. Athlete should be given a number of foot lengths to be tried by his coach.

If, for example, it is decided to use 15 foot lengths as a check mark, a baton pass will be attempted at full speed using that distance check mark. If the incoming runner passes or comes too close to the outgoing runner, then the check mark needs to be extended to perhaps 20 foot lengths, and another attempt made. If on this occasion, the incoming runner does not catch the outgoing runner, then the check mark is reduced to, 18 foot length and so on, until the baton pass is successfully carried out.

3

FUNDAMENTAL PRINCIPLES FOR RUNNERS

The undermentioned principles do not effect the performance of a runner directly but are related to it indirectly:

i. Train with Company: When starting training, runner should train with others, because this helps him to maintain interest and motivation. Train with experienced runners only, if they run at a slow pace.

Generally, experienced runners will run faster than the novice, and would be uncomfortable when running at the much slower pace with the beginner. Runner should not try to impress experienced runners by trying to stay with them in training. The end result will be that runner will run too far, too fast, too soon and develop the inevitable running injury, in particular shinsplints or a stress fracture.

ii. At first, Train Only on the Flat: Hill running stresses the quadriceps, which are usually untrained particularly in people who previously have walked only on the flat, an activity that stresses mainly the calf muscles. For this reason, it is better to walk and jog on the flat first, using muscles that are not totally untrained. Only when able to run comfortably on the flay for about 30 minutes should runner attempt hills.

iii. Learn how to Breath: Runners should learn yoga breathing, or belly breathing, which involves breathing predominantly with the diaphragm rather than with the chest muscles. With belly breathing, the chest hardly moves at all. Rather, it appears that the stomach is doing all the work; as runner breath in, his stomach goes out, and when he exhales, his stomach retracts.

Proper breathing is very important for the runner as it prevents the development of the stitch, a condition that occurs only during exercises that are undertaken in the erect posture and that involve running, jolting or both. The pain of the stitch is usually felt on the right side of the abdomen, immediately below the rib margin. Frequently, the pain is also perceived in the right shoulder joint, where it feels as if an ice pick were being driven into the joint. The pain is exacerbated by downhill running and by fast, sustained running as in short road races or time trials. Other factors that the player predispose to the development of the stitch are the lack of training, weakness of the abdominal muscles, cool weather, nervousness, starting a race too fast and eating and drinking before exercise. Player can immediately stop an attack of the stitch by lying down with his hips elevated; this also helps differentiate the stitch from other conditions, including chest pain due to heart disease. About 20 per cent of the athletes have residual discomfort on deep inspiration for 2 to 3 days after an attack of the stitch.

An alteration in breathing pattern may help relieve the stitch. Within a short period of starting a running session, breathing becomes synchronized with footfall. Thus, one automatically breathes in when landing on one leg and out when landing either on the same leg or on the opposite leg.

iv. Eat according to Feeling: All beginners need to know that the body will dictate the requirements of nutrition. Thus there is no need to follow a special diet. As an runner becomes more active, the main alteration that occur in his dietary preference are the desires to eat more carbohydrates, in particular sweets and fruits, and to increase fluid intake. These are natural responses. The carbohydrate content of the diet determines how rapidly the muscles and liver glycogen stores will be replenished after exercise, and a high-carbohydrate diet best ensures that these stores will be rapidly replaced. Fluid intake increases spontaneously to replace that which is lost in sweat and from the lungs with breathing.

Runner should drink fluid during exercise only if the exercise bout lasts more than an hour. About 500ml of fluid, cold water or a favourite refreshment, should be drunk for every hour that he run. Salt losses during short-duration exercises are relatively trivial, so it is not necessary to increase salt intake while training. There is also no need to increase protein intake, and intake of vitamins and minerals should not be increased above the extra intake that will result from the increased intake of food.

v. Weather Conditions: Runner need not to take special precaution if he wish to exercise in severe environmental conditions. For more mild conditions, it is advisable that runner should not exercise vigorously in the very early morning if the temperature is very cold.

The likelihood of developing upper respiratory tract infections seem to increase if one consistently trains very hard in very cold air.

Runner should wear rainproof clothing if it is raining heavily and a strong wind is blowing. Wind increases the windchill factor, and if runner's clothes are wet, there can develop a critical reduction in body temperature if he run too for long under such conditions.

vi. Do Regular Stretching and Strengthening Exercises: Running causes the muscles that are active to become strong and less flexible, whereas the opposing muscles that are relatively under-used become weaker. To maintain flexibility and the correct balance between opposing muscle groups, runner need to perform special exercise on a regular basis.

vii. Sleeping Time: Although the amounts of time that individuals sleep can vary quite remarkably, with some sleeping as little as 4 hours a night, the average person sleeps between 7 and 8 hours a night. With harder training the amount of time runner will need to sleep will likely increase. Many runners do not get enough sleep because they do not budge for that time taken out of the day. If they are running 2 hours a day and sleeping an extra hour every night, then they need to budget 3 hours a day for training.

Mental Strategies During Competition

In order to cultivate a positive and constructive mental dialogue during racing, each runner need to discover the specific thought and ideas that can spur them on. In time, runner will run his best when he concentrate very intensely and purposefully on what he is doing, thereby excluding all extraneous thoughts, including those relating to pain.

Experimental evidence for this has been provided by Dr. William Morgan, an exercise psychologist from University of Wisconsin. He reported a report a study that contrasted the mental strategies used during competition by a group of elite, world-class American marathon runners with the strategies used by a group of non-elite, average runners. Morgan found that during competition, the elite runners exhibited associative characteristics, that is, their thoughts were totally absorbed in the race itself. They concentrated on strategy, on staying loose, and on running as efficiently as possible by closely monitoring subtle physiological cues from their feet, calves, thighs and respiration patterns. These athletes' marathon paces were governed not by the clock, but by reading their bodies. These elite runners did not accept the concept of the marathon and precipitous falloffs in performance.

Another essential strategy used by these runners was segmenting, also called framing. With this technique, the athletes concentrated on running the race in sections without being influenced by what was still to come in the race. Thus, as they ran, they should concentrate only on holding the correct pace for the kilometre they were actually running, rather than concerning themselves with the fact that they had many more kilometres to run after that.

Importance of Training for Runners

Training to runners not only provide only physical

benefits, but mental and psychological benefits also, some of which includes the following:

i. Reduction of Tension: Tension in both normal and anxious people are reduced after vigorous exercise in both the laboratory and out of doors. Training also decreases anxiety levels and trained persons have lower levels of anxiety than nonexercisers.

Running has been used in the management of those with severe tension. Other diversional activities such as biofeedback, meditation or just quite rest are apparently equally effective, but exercise has a specific effect on a runner. When compared to a single dose of tranquillizer, a single exercise bout has a significantly greater effect on resting muscle tension. It was found in a research that exercise has a substantial acute and long-term tranquillizing effect. Runners also exhibit less tension about death than do nonrunners.

ii. Quality of Life: Athletes' quality of life improves with training. Female long-distance runners also scored higher on this scale than did nonrunners.

iii. Depression: Jogging has proved to be an effective adjunct in the treatment of depression and may be at least as effective as, and considerably cheaper than, conventional drug therapy in cases of mild depression. Cross-sectional studies show that depressive symptoms decrease with increasing levels of physical activity.

iv. Exercise and Happiness: A significant association was found between happiness and optimum physical fitness. This does not necessarily prove that exercise increases happiness. Happiness should be a factor that determines whether runner will choose to exercise or not.

v. Personality: A number of studies have focused on the effects of exercise training on personality. It has been proved that healthy adults who had exercised regularly for 4 or ore years exhibit greater energy, patience, humour, ambition and optimism and were more amiable, graceful, good-tempered, elated, and easy going than were a group of persons just commencing an exercise-training program.

Subsequent studies showed that exercise training increases self-confidence, emotional stability, self-sufficiency, conscientiousness, and persistence and reduces anxiety, tension, depression and fatigue and increases vigour.

vi. Mental Functioning: Two preliminary studies suggested that exercise training increases mental functioning, as shown by scores in a variety of tests of mathematical and other reasoning abilities; scores increased when subjects took the tests after exercising. Rats that exercise for life also show improved memory retention as they age.

Running Addiction

As the running revolution of the 1970s took hold and the literature describing its benefits grew, it was only natural that a counter literature should develop. The major contention of this countermovement was that running is detrimental because it is addictive. Researchers have described the criteria that should be fulfilled for a diagnosis of exercise dependence. One definition states that addiction occurs when involvement in an activity eliminates choice in all areas of life. On this basis, an addiction must be distinguished from a habit, commitment or compulsion, none of which exclude all other activities.

Sacks has found that running addiction usually starts during a period of increased emotional stress. In this regard, running is especially attractive because it is an easy skill to acquire and therefore provides a simple and rapid solution to emotional distress.

Nutritional Requirement of Runners

There are basically three rules of nutrition:

First, the body requires essential nutrients, namely, carbohydrates, proteins and fats and the vitamins, minerals, trace elements and water that are necessary for the utilization of that energy;

Second, these nutrients are contained in four basic food groups, namely, meat, fish, and meat-substitute group, the fruits and vegetable group; the milk and dairy produce group and the bread and cereal group;

Third, the items from these four basic food groups should be eaten in the following portions each day:

Cereal - 4 portion

Fruits and vegetable - 4 portion.

Basic Nutrients

Following are considered to be the fundamental components of nutrients:

a. Protein: There are few dietary myths greater than those surrounding the protein needs of people who exercise vigorously. Most people are aware that strength-trained athletes, in particular power lifters and weight lifters, have an ability to eat protein in the form of eggs and meat that defines description.

Protein is a relatively minor fuel during exercise; only during prolonged exercise in the carbohydrate-depleted state to proteins become more important. Even then, protein supplies only about 10 per cent of the total energy requirement and is used as a substrate both for new glucose production in the liver and for oxidation in the Krebs cycle.

Nevertheless, the increased use of proteins during

exercise may be sufficient to increase the daily dietary protein requirements of runners to about twice. The main function of body protein stores is to provide the basic structure of most body tissues, in particular the muscle proteins actin and myosin, as well as other essential components such as hormones, cellular that is, they are continually being broken down and replaced by new proteins protein turnover rate and equals about 25g of protein per day for a 70-kg person. Stresses such as physical training, severe illness, or major surgery will lead to an increased protein turnover training, severe illness, or major surgery all lead to turnover acts mainly as a noncarbohydrate source of new glucose, especially when the rate of carbohydrate utilization during exercise exceeds the rate of dietary carbohydrate digestion so that body carbohydrate stores fall. It is apparent that these demands for more protein arise from within the body. It is not possible to increase the body's protein metabolism artificially and thereby stimulate muscle growth simply by eating larger amounts of protein in the diet.

b. Carbohydrate: This constituent plays a very important role in diet of a runner. The main considerations in this respect are:

Carbohydrate containing foods: Some high-carbohydrate foods, all of which comprise at least 90 per cent carbohydrate with less than 5 per cent protein and 5 per cent fat, are potatoes, rice, macaroni, jams, oranges, grapes, carrots, white bread, and crispbread. These are the types of carbohydrate containing foods that should be eaten during heavy training.

A high-carbohydrate diet consists almost exclusively

of fruits, vegetables, and cereals. Sweets, chocolates and other confectioneries may have relatively lower carbohydrate contents because of high fat contents. It is best to eat more natural high-carbohydrate foot, in particular potatoes, during carbohydrate loading.

Carbohydrate Depletion Diet: Highly trained athletes should not undergo the carbohydrate-depletion prolonged exercise, especially exercise that lasts more than 4 hours. By providing the carbohydrate-depletion phase, they also avoid some potential dangers. Less well trained runners may benefit from the carbohydrate-depletion phase.

Using this technique, they may store more muscle and liver glycogen than they would be only eating a high-carbohydrate diet for the last 3 days before competition. For this reason, it is always advised to modify carbohydrate-depletion diet before a major race.

c. Water: Water is very important for the runner during training, as most of the water from his body brings out in the form of sweat. Thus, athlete should take water in appropriate quantity. What is this appropriate quantity depends on weather conditions, i.e., runner performing in hot weathers have to take more water than runner performing in cold weather.

However, athlete should not take the water in excess quantity which is required as more consumption of it will create a problem for the athlete in running.

d. Minerals: The most important mineral in the diet include:

potassium, iron, zinc, copper, sodium and calcium.

i. Iron: Exercise, running particular, causes increased iron losses from the body. Because the daily intake of iron, especially in females, is only marginally above the levels needed to balance normal daily iron losses, the additional iron losses caused by running may cause iron deficiency. Runners most likely to become iron deficient are those who run high weekly mileages, women runners who lose large amounts of blood diets.

Foods that have a high-iron content include liver, red meat, egg yolk, legumes, dark green leafy vegetables, molasses, and whole grains. Vegetarians who eat no meat or eggs are particularly prone to iron deficiency. All at-risk runners could benefit by eating more red meat, liver or the dark meat of fowls, and some should take iron tablets if their blood haemoglobin levels are found to be sufficiently low to indicate iron deficiency anaemia. Daily iron requirements of heavily training runners might be as much as 2 mg, but because only 10 per cent of ingested iron is actually absorbed, one should aim to ingest about 20 mg of iron per day. The diet normally provides about 6 mg of iron per 1000 kcal of energy. Thus, a normal dietary intake of 3000 kcal will provide 18 mg of iron, which should be sufficient to balance daily iron losses exceed 2 mg.

Athlete should keep in his mind that iron tablets have some drawbacks, while iron is best absorbed when taken with foods high in vitamin C. Tea and Coffee greatly diminish iron absorption, as do the oxalates, phyates, and phosphates found in whole-grain food. By simple drinking orange juice and not tea or coffee with meals, one can increase the iron absorbed from a meal fivefold.

Similarly, animal protein increases from absorption from beans and peas.

ii. Sodium: Sodium is stored mainly in the body fluids with much smaller amounts inside cells. Sodium plays a number of important physiological roles:

a. It maintains the normal water balance and distribution within the body;

b. It determines the blood pressure; and

c. It maintains osmotic equilibrium, acid-base balance, and normal muscular irritability. Total body sodium content is about 80 g.

It has been proved that body's daily salt requirement is about 0.2 to 0.5 g about one tenth of what we actually consume. The excess that is ingested is lost in the urine. Even vigorous and prolonged daily exercise increase salt requirements only very slightly, because sweat has a low-salt content that decreases as one becomes more fit and heat acclimatized. Thus, the sweat of heat-acclimatized runners has a very low salt content, so that its composition approaches that of distilled water. The salt content of sweat in an untrained subject is about 3.5 g of salt per litre of sweat, whereas the sweat of a trained subject contains about 1.8 of salt per litre of sweat. This implies that untrained subjects would have to sweat a minimum of 3 litre per day and trained athlete up to 6 litres per day just to rid themselves of the excess salt in their bodies. To induce salt deficits, they would need to exercise even more.

iii. Magnesium: In some countries, magnesium level in the soil and therefore also in the drinking and irrigation water are low. Persons living in these areas may well have mild magnesium deficiencies, symptoms of which may include impaired exercise tolerance.

iv. Potassium: Potassium is used in the body mainly inside the cells and is found in the diet of citrus fruits, bananas, and tomatoes. The daily potassium requirement is about 2 to 4 g, which is bout 4 to 8 times more than the daily salt requirement. The total body potassium store is also about 90 g. During exercise, potassium is lost in urine and sweat, but these loses are trivial. Thus sweat potassium content is only 0.1 to 0.2 g/L; even when eating a low-potassium diet, subjects exercising at 50 per cent VO2 max for 2 hours a day in the heat showed no evidence of developing potassium deficiency. The major factor for runners is that potassium is stored with glycogen in the body; hence, potassium requirements are increased during carbohydrate loading.

The ingestion of fruit during carbohydrate loading will adequately cover the additional potassium needs. The potassium stored with glycogen is released into the bloodstream as exercise progresses and as the intramuscular glycogen stores are utilized. The extra potassium is then lost in sweat and urine in place of sodium chloride; thus, potassium excretion during exercise helps to conserve sodium.

v. Zinc: The possibility that distance runners may be zinc deficient was raised by a study in which blood zinc levels are found to be low in a group of runners and lowest in those who trained the hardest. The symptoms of zinc deficiency are:

Loss of taste and smell,

Loss of appetite;

Loss of hair; and

Skin lesions.

Zinc is found mainly in protein foods, and its content is low in high-carbohydrate foods such as fruit, vegetables, grains and pasta; thus, vegetarian runners are more likely to be zinc deficient.

vi. Calcium: Most of the body's calcium stores exist in bone and the major complication of calcium deficiency is reduced bone strength due to inadequate bone calcification. The only athlete likely to be at risk of calcium deficiencies are those females whose diets are abnormal, particularly those whose eating patterns preclude them from eating an adequate amount of dairy products, the major source of dietary calcium.

e. Fats: Fat in the diet provides a convenient, palatable, and highly concentrated source of energy. Triglyceride is the form in which fat occurs both in food and in the body's fat stores. The principal foods contributing fat to the diet are vegetable oil, salad dressing, meat, the visible fat of meat, the skin of chicken, egg yolk, nuts, olives, avocados, and dairy produce such as milk, cream, cheese and butter. These fats may be either saturated or unsaturated.

Ideal Diet for Runners

Many studies have undergone on the topic of ideal diet of runners and diet resulted from overall studies is that the optimum athletic diet should include 55 per cent of energy from carbohydrate, 30 per cent from fat and 15 per cent from protein. Ideally, 350 to 500 of carbohydrates should be eaten daily.

4

RULES OF RUNNING

MIDDLE-DISTANCE RUNNING

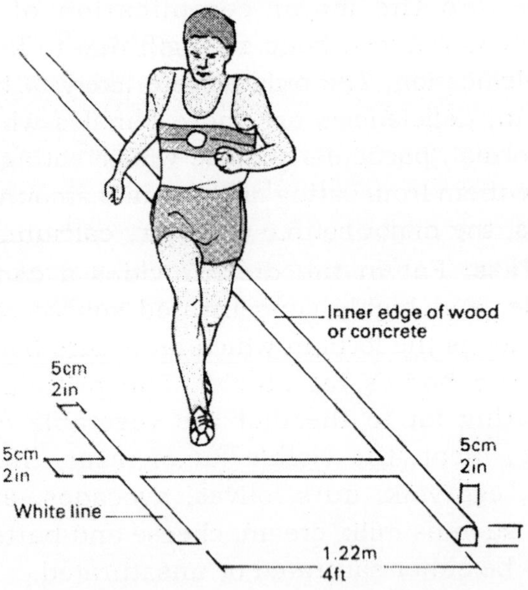

Start

i. The start and finish shall be indicated by a line 0.05 m. in width. In all races not run in lanes the starting line shall be curved so that all the runners start the same distance from the finish.

ii. The starting for all races will be the report of a pistol.

iii. For all races up to and including 400 m. the words

of the starter shall be "On your marks", "Set", and when all competitors are steady, the pistol shall be fired. In races longer than 400 m., the words shall be "On your marks" and when all competitors are steady, the pistol shall be fired.

iv. If, for any reason, the starter is not satisfied that all are ready, he or she shall order the competitors to stand up.

a. In all races up to and including 400 m. where a crouch start must be used, both hands must be in contact with the ground when the competitor is in the "Set" position.

b. On the command "On your marks" or "Set" as the case may be, all competitors shall at once and without delay assume their full and final "Set" position. Failure to comply with this command after a reasonable time shall constitute a false start.

c. Competitors must not touch either the start line or the ground in front of it with their hands or feet when on their marks.

d. If a competitor, after the command "On your marks", disturbs the other competitors in the race through sound or otherwise, it may be considered a false start.

e. If a competitor leaves his or her marks with hand or foot after the words "On your marks" or "Set" as the case may be, and before the report of the pistol it shall be considered a false start.

f. Any competitor making a false start must be warned and will be disqualified if he or she is responsible for a second false start.

g. If in the opinion of the Starter, the start was not fair, he or she shall recall the competitors by firing a pistol.

v. Starting blocks must be used for all races up to and including 400 metres (including the first leg of the 4×200 m. and 4×400 m. Relays) but may not be used for any other race.

Finish

i. Competitors shall be placed in the order in which their "torso" (as distinguished from head, neck, arms, legs, hands or feet) reaches the vertical plane of the nearer edge of the finish line.

ii. Two white posts shall be positioned 30 cm. from the edge of the track to denote the extremities of the finish line.

iii. In races decided on the basis of the distance covered in a fixed period of time, the Starter shall fire the pistol exactly one minute before the end of the race to alert competitors and judges that the race is nearing its end. As the pistol is then fired at the exact time to end the race, the judge (one for each competitor) must mark the spot of the last footprint of the competitor at the report of the pistol.

Running in Lanes: In all races run in lanes, competitors must stay within their assigned lane from start to finish. If a competitor is forced outside his or her lane by another competitor and no material advantage is gained, the competitor shall not be disqualified.

Scoring: Unless otherwise agreed upon by the competing teams, the number of team points allotted for place finish is as follows:

—Two teams with 2 competitors in each event: 5, 3, 2, 1.

-Three teams with 2 competitors in each event: 7, 5, 4, 3, 2, 1.

-Two teams with 3 competitors in each event: 7, 5, 4, 3, 2, 1.

-Six teams with 1 competitor in each event: 7, 5, 4, 3, 2, 1.

—Relay races with 2 teams: 5, 2.

Relay races with 3 teams: 7, 4, 2.

Relay races with 6 teams: 7, 5, 4, 3, 2, 1.

Obstructions: Any competitor jostling or obstructing another competitor is subject to disqualification. If any act of disqualification affects the performance of another competitor, the Referee may order the race to be re-held excluding the violator or may permit the offended competitor to compete in a subsequent round of the race.

STEEPLECHASE

a. The standard distances are: 300 m. and 2000 m. (Junior events only).

b. There are 28 hurdle jumps and 7 water jumps included in the 3000 m. event and 18 hurdle jumps and 5 water jumps in the 2000 m. event.

c. The water jump shall be the fourth jump in each lap.

d. The distance from the start to the beginning of the first lap should not include any jumps, the hurdles being removed until competitors have entered the first lap.

e. The exact length of laps or the precise position of the water jump cannot be specified since the water jump must be constructed inside or, preferably outside the track which will lessen or lengthen the standard distance of the laps. The two essential guidelines to be followed are: (1) There must be enough distance from the starting line to the first hurdle to prevent overcrowding and (2) There should be approximately 68 m. from the last hurdle to the finish line.

f. The hurdles shall be 0.914 m. high and at least 3.96 m. in width. The top bar shall be 127 mm. square. The weight of the hurdle and supporting base should be adequate to provide stability for runners to step on top of the hurdle.

g. The competitor may jump or vault over each hurdle or place a foot on the hurdles.

h. The water jump should be 3.66 m. in length and width.

i. The water should be level with the track surface and 0.70 m. deep at the hurdle end and slope upward to the level of the track at the farther end.

ii. Each competitor must go over or through the water.

RELAY RACES

a. The course for Relay Races should be marked with lines 50 mm. wide to designate the distances of the four stages of the race and to denote the scratch line.

b. It is permissible in relay races for a competitor to

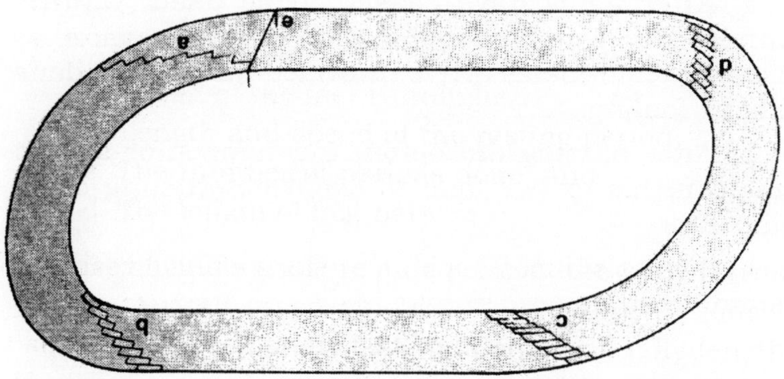

make a check mark within his or her own lane.

c. Lines 50 mm. wide should also be drawn 10 m. before and after the scratch line to denote the take-over (exchange) zone. The baton must be passed within the exchange zone. The lines are included within the zone.

i. In races up to 4×200 m., the runners (other than the first runner) may start their run not more than 10 m. outside the exchange zone. A mark should be made in each lane to denote this extended limit.

ii. All relay races are not restricted to lanes from start to finish, but rather, at varying distances, only portions of the race must be in designated lanes.

d. The baton must be carried in the hand throughout the race and must be passed (not thrown) within the exchange zone.

e. If the baton is dropped, it must be recovered by the competitor who dropped it.

f. The baton is considered passed when it is in the hand of the receiving runner. In regard to the exchange zone, it is the position of the baton which is decisive, and not the position of the body or limbs of the competitors.

g. After lanes have ceased to be used, waiting runners are free to move to an inner position as incoming team-mates arrive, provided this can be done without fouling.

h. After passing the baton, the competitor should remain in his or her lane to avoid obstructing other competitors.

i. Any assistances such as pushing-off will result in disqualification.

ROAD RACES

a. The standard distances for men and women shall be 15 km, 20 km, Half Marathon, 25 km, 30 km and

Marathon Race (42.195 km).

b. The race may be run over a variety of surfaces such as regular streets and roads or, if duly marked, bicycle or foot paths but not on soft ground. Care must be taken to ensure the safety of the competitors and, where possible, provisions should be made to close the roads to traffic.

c. The distance in kilometres on the route shall be displayed to all the competitors.

d. Refreshments shall be provided by the organizers of races over 20 km at approximately every 5 km.

i. Refreshments which may be provided by the competitors themselves or by the organizers at the designated stations shall be easily accessible for the competitors or they may actually be put into the hands of the competitor.

ii. In addition to the refreshment stations, sponging points, where only water is supplied, shall be provided midway between refreshment stations.

iii. Refreshments are not to be taken any place other than the points designated.

Selection of Appropriate Running Shoes

Once the runner has go-ahead to start running, the next step for him is to choose an appropriate pair of running shoes. This is easier said than done. These days, it has become quite difficult to select the appropriate shoes as number of varieties of shoes are now available in the market.

Choice of Shoes

It is always advisable for the beginning runners to start running in a relatively modestly priced pair of shoes, bought from a reputable running shoe dealer. If after some months of running, runner get injured, the nature of injury will indicate what type of shoe is likely to help cure that injury and prevent further similar injuries.

Runner should take a lot of care while selecting his shoes as this effects his performance to a greater extent.

Features of Running Shoe

Any running shoe has six major features, namely:

i. Mid-sole;

ii. Outer sole;

iii. Heel counter;

iv. Presence or absence of slip lasting; and

v. Lateral midsole heel flares.

Mid-Sole: The mid-sole is the real heart of the shoe and is the feature of the shoe which a runner should notice very carefully. The most important feature of this mid-sole is the degree of softness or hardness. The midsole has three different functions:

It must absorb the shock of the heel strike and the forefoot strike;

It must be strong enough to resist excessive inward rotation of the ankle as the foot progresses from heel strike to toe-off; and

It must be able to flex at a point about two thirds from the heel as the heel starts to come off the ground leading to toe-off.

In the earlier days, mid-sole material was made only from rubber, which has dual disadvantages of being heavy and a relatively poor absorber of shock. Another problem arises from the manufacturing process; it is difficult to produce EVA of consistent hardness. As a result, the quality of the mid-sole can vary from shoe to shoe. For these reasons, it is essential to compare the middle hardness of all the shoes for which thumb compression test is considered a good method.

Basically, the features of the midsole that require consideration are its hardness and whether or not it is made of mixed material. Those who require shock absorption in their running shoes because they have rigid lower-lib structure must look for shoes with soft midsoles; those with mobile feet need firmer shoes.

Outer Sole: The outer sole is that part of the shoe that comes into direct contact with the ground. Today, outer soles are made from a variety of different materials and are of different designs. The main design variation is whether or not the sole has waffles. Waffles were originally designed for cross-country races, not for road races, because they give better traction on uneven ground and they also increase absorption.

However, waffles do not wear as well as flat-surfaced outer shoes. The most important feature of outer sole is that it should not wear down too quickly. It should have the greatest durability in the areas of greatest wear, particularly at the outer heel edge. This type of outer sole has been called the nonuniform outer sole. Very durable material is not used throughout the entire outer sole. Thus, the nonuniform outer sole saves weight.

The only benefit of a soft and therefore nondurable outer sole is that it provides additional cushioning, which may be useful to those runners for whom exceptional shock absorption is essential. Thus, the important features of the outer sole are durability and traction.

Heelcounter: The heel counter is made from a firm thermoplastic material that is moulded into the correct shape during a special heating process. Some heel counters extend further on the inner than on the outer side of the shoe, and these days most are associated with special stabilizing structures that tend to bind the heel counter more firmly to the midsole. The aim of the heel counter is to reduce ankle pronation.

The athlete who requires a shoe that will limit ankle pronation should obviously choose a shoe with a strong heel counter. There are two ways to test the strength of the heel counter:

First, pinch the middle of the heel counter on its inner and outer edges between the thumb and the index and second fingers of dominant hand. Determine how much pressure is required to distort the heel counter towards the centre of the shoe;

Secondly, holding the heel counter as before, grasp the midsole of the shoe in the palm of the other hand and determine how much torque is required to distort the heel counter to the inside or to the outside of the shoe.

The less distortion produced by these manoeuvres, the stronger the heel counter.

Presence or Absence of Slip Lasting: During the construction of running shoes, the nylon material that constitutes the shoe upper, the part that covers the top of the foot, is stitched together, and its lower part is glued onto the top of the midsole. If this part of the upper is stuck directly to the midsole and no additional material overlies it, the shoe is said to be slip lasted.

If a brown-coloured board overlies and hides the tucked-under portion of the upper, the shoes is said to be board lasted. Board lasting increases the ability of the shoe to resist pronation. The board may extend from heel to toe, in which case the board lasting is conventional, or the board may end just behind the ball of the foot, in which case it is called partial or combination lasting.

The benefit of partial board lasting is that it does not reduce flexibility in the forefoot yet retains some ability to resist ankle pronation. In general, board-lasted shoes will benefit those runners who require shoes that control excessive ankle pronation, whereas slip-lasted shoes are best for those with rigid feet that require as much movement as possible.

Later Midsole Heel Flares: The mid-sole of the shoe at the heel is usually wider on both sides where it meets the ground than where it meets the foot; in other words it is flared from foot to ground. The flare on the inside of the shoe probably resists ankle pronation; the flare on the outside probably increases ankle pronation because it acts as a lever forcing the foot inward at the heel strike. Thus, it seems likely that the medial feel flare may be of value to runners who need control of ankle pronation, but the lateral flare is probably more of a hindrance than a help to these runners.

Final Decision

After deciding which shoes to buy, runner should make himself satisfied that his shoe fulfils the following requirements:

a. The width of the shoe must be right, and there must be sufficient height in the toe box to allow free up-and-down movement of the toes. Athletes with very wide or very narrow feet will need to look for manufacturers whose normal width ranges tend to be either broader or narrower than the average running shoe. The most important width fitting is over the middle of the foot;

b. The heel must not slip out of the heel counter at toe-off;

c. The shoe must feel good at the time of being purchase. A shoe that feels uncomfortable in the shop will only become even more so once on the road;

d. The shoe should be fitted in the afternoon and should be slightly larger than conventional shoes. This is because, runner's foot will swell about one half size during the day and during running. The width of his index finger should be able to fit between the end of the longest toe and the front end of the shoe upper.

Running Clothes

The key to choose appropriate running clothes is to dress lightly when running. In most countries, during the summer, a pair of shorts and a T-shirt are all that the runner should use. When it is not, he should wear only the lightest, most porous clothing. This is because when running, runner's body will produce an enormous amount of heat and he will experience great difficulty in losing that heat. The tendency when exercising in mild to warm conditions is to overheat, and wearing a track suit during exercise will only exaccerbate this.

Runner is advised to wear a track suit only when the temperature is near 0 degree, when a strong, cold wind is blowing or when he is trying to acclimatize to hot-weather running. Beginning runners should exercise in track suits in the mistaken belief that they will lose more weight that way. This is not true.

Exercising in a track suit simply causes runner to sweat more. The only way to lose real body weight with exercise is to burn more calories of energy, and this is achieved only by doing more exercise. Even then the amount of weight lost may be quite disappointing, if he does not follow a fairly strict diet in addition to exercise.